Woods, An Art

A collection of Poetry Classics - Vol X – Vol VIX

A Diamond Collection

Jane Summers

AuthorHouse™
1663 Liberty Drive
Bloomington, IN 47403
www.authorhouse.com
Phone: 833-262-8899

Because of the dynamic nature of the Internet, any web addresses or links contained in this book may have changed
since publication and may no longer be valid. The views expressed in this work are solely those of the author and do
not necessarily reflect the views of the publisher, and the publisher hereby disclaims any responsibility for them.

Any people depicted in stock imagery provided by Getty Images are models,
and such images are being used for illustrative purposes only.
Certain stock imagery © Getty Images.

This book is printed on acid-free paper.

ISBN: 978-1-6655-1934-2 (sc)
ISBN: 978-1-6655-1933-5 (e)

Library of Congress Control Number: 2021904726

Print information available on the last page.

Published by AuthorHouse 03/23/2021

CONTENTS

WOODS AN ART, WINTER
A collection of Poems: Vol XI: A Poetry Classic 54

WOODS AN ART, SPRING

WOODS AN ART, SUMMER

A Collection of Poems: Vol XIII: A Poetry Classic

WOODS, AN ART, WINTER

A Collection of Poems: Vol IIX: A poetry Classic

ACKNOWLEDGEMENTS

This book is dedicated to my father Dr. Chinta Chidananda Rao, my mother Chinta Visalakshi, my husband Srinivas Madiraju, my daughter Anika Madiraju, my brother, and sisters.

A special tribute to all my friends who helped me in time of need.

Woods, an Art, is a collection of 5 poetry classics, prayers of gratitude, lyrics of Jane Summer's song, Summer Sunrise, and Durvouve a dictionary of new language, Durvue and new English words.

I am Durga Madiraju, and I write under the pen name of Jane Summers.

Woods an Art, is a diamond collection, and contains poems with new English words, new language Durvue, and new language dictionary Durvouve***, to grace a lifetime – Jane Summers.***

FOREWORD

Poetry classic X contains 25 poems, and the poems are about sunrise, early, a bud on a tree, rocks for a difference of a mountain and ocean, sunrise, sunset for a difference of colors, ocean waves for colors of sunrise and sunset, droopy a poise, a cheer I need for my flowers, vases of flowers, a difference of my trees to sit in, and others.

Poetry Classic XI contains 25 poems, and the poems are about clusters of flowers for a difference of a color, poise of seasons for a grace, hidden petals of inner flowers for a new flower, petals torn of breeze for a new shape, leaves a pattern, a difference of seasons dances and others.

Poetry Classic XII contains 25 poems, and the poems are patternlet poems distinguished from one object to another, for a difference of a line, a spot, a jagged edge with crevices, a shade or others for a new pattern, and others.

Poetry Classic XIII contains 25 poems and are abstract poems defined and related through a thematic text to relate an abstraction to a context of another object, for a definition, detail, relation or others.

Poetry Classic XIV contains 15 poems, and the poems have new English words used to describe season's nature such as flowers, festivals, autumn breeze, autumn celebration and others. The meanings of the new English words are given at the end of the book, along with usage, to define an example sentence.

Poetry Classic XV contains 1 poem, and the poem is written using a new language, Durvue. The words in the poem are derived from the new language, and portray nature through flowers, leaves, trees, and others. The new language, Durvue, defines words, nouns, verbs, and others used to write the poem.

Part 2 of the book contains lyrics of Jane Summers, for the song, Sunrise Summer, a vocal.

Part 3 contains new words, (Durvouve) derived from the new language durvue. The new words are defined through a dictionary of words, with meaning and usage for the new language at the end of each poem.

PREFACE

Sunrise, a journey of miles of art, I traverse, a sky until night, a new art!

Sunrise early is an art, a blob, a few minutes a bud, a tree until sunrise mid-morning, a flower a tree, a visitor, a few minutes!

Sunrise, an iris, a flower, a few minutes, until sunrise petal lines several in the sky!

Several blobs, my sunrise, my sky, until a mid-morning!

Sunrise, a white, several splashes, my sky, until noon!

Sunrise, a journey, a white and blue sky to match my ocean waves, until sunset!

Sunset, a journey, a white, now a slight yellow and a slight orange, a mid-afternoon!

Sunset, a journey of an orange and a light grey, until sunset late, to a night of a few stars, my visitors, my canvas!

Sunset a journey, an end, a dark canvas, for a night now!

Black, a canvas my sky, now only a sky of stars, a journey for time!

My skies at night, a moon, a slight white and blue, a sun blob?

A journey of night, moon a few days, a yellow, and a slight white, and stars a path, a difference for time, until morning!

Night, my canvas, a dance of stars, several a path, moon a yellow round, a visitor a few days a month, a moon-star dance an art, dances, arrangements, several!

A bouquet of flowers, an arrangement for a sentiment, a tradition, until a name new, a new significance!

Poise, a grace, an art, seasons, for a dress, a grace, a conversation, a harmony, or any, for a comfort, every and any!

Petals, hidden a flower, until a learning, ready. A shape, a fold new of a day for a journey, a lifetime!

WOODS, A SPRING WEAVE SILVER

A Collection of Poems: A Poetry Classic Vol X

Jane Summers

1. *Petals, a Pattern!*

Petals,

A texture, a flower

A pattern true!

Lighter, a petal,

Faint my lines,

A pattern, true!

A petal,

A texture, a velvet,

Darker, a shade,

wide, a border!

A petal,

A difference

An angle, a shape,

A curve, an edge sharp

A flower, a pattern!

Petals,

Lines softer,

A texture, a mum,

Lines very faint, several!

A fold inner, a line!

A pattern, a daisy!

Petals are a pattern, any a flower!

2. *An art for a mood!*

An art,

My mood, today,

A cheer of summer!

A joy, my day!

Colors, Flowers, Nature, my art!

An art,

A pensive mood

For I ponder,

A day of clouds, an art, I carve!

Colors, I look at,

For an abstraction,

A learning, an abstract art!

An abstraction of an artlet true!

An art for an abstraction, a learning new!

3. *A disturbance, A disarray!*

A disturbance, a disarray,

My art,

My dress,

My voice!

Not any,

An appeal!

A day to recapture,

A calmness of mind, for peace,

A work for a focus,

Smiles for a cheer,

To learn from my work,

A need!

An appreciation, I need!

Joys of a few,

A reward,!,

A disarray afore,

Now a poise of grace,

A friend I earned!

A reward, an appreciation for a task not a disarray!

4. *A sunrise, a bud!*

A sunrise sun, a bud on a tree,

Time a value,

White, my light, my day,

Only to traverse a sky,

A morning until sunset!

A difference of night

A blue to disappear, a sunset,

A few clouds, a deep blue,

An orange grey, my sunset!

A sunrise sun, a bud for time until a

sky white and blue, a sky!

5. *Sunrise, An Iris*

Sunrise,

An iris my flower, sunrise,

Only to move away for time,

A line silver, now!

Several lines, a blue!

My silver lining, my sunrise!

Days of

Silver lining,

Days, I wear a blue, white, a badge, true!

A value of my hard work,

Appreciated, any!

Sunrise, a silver lining, days of hard work, appreciated,

a difference of value, my work, a silver lining!

6. *Rocks, a difference of a mountain*

A rock,

A purpose,

A decor, an ocean,

A difference of a rock, a land,

A difference, a color, a shape, a size!

Sunrise,

Time for a difference of colors!

Sunset, colors, hidden,

A view of a rock, a difference of a mountain!

Colors, many, a rock,

Time, a path forward!

A difference of a rock,

A tide!

A difference of,

A sunrise, sunset,

My rocks!

A rock a new name, a difference, a pattern!

A difference of a rock, land and ocean, time, a new name!

7.   Sunrise, sunset a difference!

Sunrise

A shade lighter a sunset,

Flowers, a color pale!

White a blend!

Flowers, sunset, Awake,

A difference, a shade, Nights!

Deeper, A night warm,

Seasons?

Ocean waves,

Colors, a difference,

Of a day!

Flowers, sunrise, sunset, a difference of a pale and a deep bloom.

8. *Waves, colors a sunrise and sunset!*

Clouds, my mountains,

A morning of clouds,

A blue and grey!

A red and yellow,

A sunrise summer!

A pink and orange,

A sunset summer!

A color,

Only a blue and grey,

A blue and white,

A match my ocean!

Mountains, colors a difference of seasons,

similar an ocean blue, grey and white all!

9. *Petals, a flower inside!*

Petals new,

Only to grow inside, a flower!

A peony, a shape!

A color, a season,

A petal, an inner, a home!

Petals, awake,

A rose,

A mum!

A poise,

A grace, to sit in!

A tree, a vase,

My home!

For I

Now know,

How to sit gracefully,

On a stem!

10. *Droopy, A cheer for my flowers!*

Droopy my flowers,

Dusky and gloomy,

A day, a season!

Autumn or winter?

Water and food, flowers awake,

Smiles, my flowers!

A sunshine smile, true!

Yellow and white, my lights,

A dance of my flowers!

Droopiness, not any!

My words for a difference,

A cheer true, my words,

My sunrise light,

A difference!

Days of gloom, not any!

A droopy flower, not now,

Only a cheer, true!

11.   *A Flower, hidden!*

Flowers hidden,

A color, an age,

Hidden for years,

Tree, my home!

My tree now,

Flowers,

Many a color,

My sisters,

I whisper to,

for a conversation!

12. *An autumn breeze, fierce!*

Trees,

A learning seasons!

An autumn,

My hidden flowers,

Only to seek,

More a cover!

Petals,

I protect, dew and mist,

An autumn safe,

Not missed!

My autumn breeze,

My petals thick and deep,

An autumn cover,

My shelter!

13. *Vases, my trees!*

A vase,

To sit in

My tree leaves!

Seasons, Spring and Summer!

Empty branches, a winter

Dry stems, my vase!

Branches, a decoration,

My backyard!

My azalea flowers,

A spring vase,

My tree,

I decorate,

My front meadows,

Every year!

A few days,

My visitor,

My azaleas,

I await,

For a splendor!

A hurry,

I need to match,

My peaches,

Lemons,

Oranges,

And bananas,

A vase my tree, fruits, true!

An arrangement of

My azaleas and fruits

A vase, my meadows!

My flowers and fruits, I need to match

for my azalea flowers, my tree vase!

14. *Sunrise sunset similar*

Sunrise,

A match of sunset,

Time, true,

A trait, color,

Words,

A smile, a shade!

Anger, deeper a sunset orange!

Deeper, a sky blue!

Sunrise, colors,

Lighter,

My words, smiles,

Lighter, a tea color!

Lighter, my step,

Lighter, a sunrise dance true!

My dress, a color, pale, a sunrise,

A white, a blue, a pink, a lemon!

My days of sunrise colors, a cheer!

Only a joy, true!

Sunset colors,

For an autumn cheer,

Similar, a sunrise sky,

Colors, a step, an indent,

A foot print, I match,

Lest I fall,

Colors orange, purple, green, dark pink,

Petals heavy,

Velvets, satins,

My dress and step, a decor of autumn, true!

15. *A day of difference*

A day of difference,

I know now,

A tree, several branches,

Leaves and flowers,

Seasons,

A Spring, summer, true!

A tree empty,

A mid-autumn, a winter true!

A day of difference,

Knowledge, a learning,

Days and nights,

I study and work!

A togetherness, my harmony!

My, Learning,

My knowledge,

My art,

I know seasons,

For a difference,

Of a tree,

A flower,

Buds, leaves

And every!

A knowledge, a difference of seasons, true!

16. *Knowledge, I Cherish!*

Empty

Of a sky gloomy,

Not any, an art of sunshine!

Empty my branches, afore,

Now, smiles only,

Seasons All!

My knowledge,

I cherish,

Treasure and Share!

A joy, cheer true,

My family,

Only smiles,

A knowledge, a use, every, not a branch empty!

My branches, before empty, now my learning deep!

17. *My tea art!*

My tea art,

I create new, every!

For a day of sunshine!

A learning, to match an age!

A tea art, true!

A learning spring,

My linen, my tea,

Pale, my colors!

A light pink rose, my tea set!

My tea fragrance,

A lavender,

A rose,

A chamomile!

My tea, a winter,

A poinsetta, a burgundy red!

Gold and red my tea set!

My learning,

A match,

My Winter tea, deep!

A bergmont oil, my tea fragrance!

A tea art pattern, to learn a summer and winter, for a learning of health!

18. Trees on Rocks

Rocks with foliage,

Rocks with sloppy meadows,

And rocks on ocean,

An orange puddle dirt,

A need?

A sunrise and sunset colors, a puddle, a need?

I need to wash my sunrise sunset puddle,

A rain, a need!

Rocks made up of foliage, mossy grass, and

dirt, I need to clean for a need!

19. Rocks, shapes!

A shape of a rock,

An artifact, any!

A shape, many!

Color, several,

An abstract rock, true!

A shape a rock, a water pattern,

Serene a pattern, calm!

A calmness for no tide!

I need to watch,

For a change,

A sunset, true!

Rocks, shapes, several, a shape a difference a tide, sunrise, sunset!

20. *A bridge without a railing, a fence?*

A bridge,

A river under,

A step,

I can't miss!

To count a step, a need!

A step, I need to complete!

All steps

Only for a cross over!

My days of hard work,

I read and gather for a year!

A result,

A showing,

One time!

A success?

A year,

An appreciation, true!

A failure, not any!

A step one, success until an end, only a

step better for a goal fulfilled and met!

21.   *A surprise friend!*

Alone, a dusk

I read a book,

An abstraction,

For a comfort!

I need, a winter!

A friend

Unaware, outside,

A sunset dusk!

Snow, ice, outside!

A curtain,

I move a little!

A surprise!

A hand extended!

Several branches, My tree, outside!

Leaning towards me!

A friendship true, this winter!

A friendship, a difference of a tree and a sunset dusk

22. *My cold, I nurse!*

Flowers,

Leaves,

To nurse my cold and cough,

My breathing,

Only for a breeze calm!

My milk and pepper,

My euclyaptus oil,

Every winter,

I inhale, a drop in water,

A need, true

My cold, not any, now!

I nurse my cold, with soups, and euclypatus oil drop every winter!

23. *Sunrise, a path I traverse!*

Sunrise,

A canvas for time, colors!

A sunrise,

I need to pray,

Kartika deepam, a deepam,

Days, a lamp I light, early dawn!

Nights, a lamp I light, an early dusk!

Until,

A Karthika masam, a season

An end, a year!

A Karthik masam, a full moon, a month,

I await,

To perform,

My satyanarayana swami pooja!

Holy and auspicious,

Only a Karthika masam!

Blessings, prosperity, my family!

My Goddess Parvati,

Only to bestow a gift!

Wishes, peace!

Harmony, living, every!

In any an endeavor!

A sunrise, sun, true?

A sunset dusk orange, true?

A Karthika pournami day, true?

I pray day and night, a karthika month, my

karthika masam prayers of peace!

24.   *A friend, I Await!*

A friend,

Nights, long,

awake,

Tired,

Only for a need of help!

My friend,

I need to nurse,

A health!

Only for a summer sky,

White!

Roses, pink, smiles!

voice, a melody, a cuckoo,

A laughter, sweet!

A step,

A dance clear,

skies!

Only more graceful!

A sunrise,

I await every winter

For a summer!

My friend,

My cuckoo!

To greet me, every year,

Every sunrise, a cheer I need!

My friend, awake, healthy,

A spring, a joy!

My friend I need to nurse, a winter!

25. *Lilies, a line faint!*

Lilies,

Long, wide!

Seasons,

Colors, pale!

A shade, an outer,

An inner, a dark,

A match!

A sunrise line, colors!

An indent, a petal inner,

Several indents!

Several lines, my petal lines!

My lilies, lines faint, a petal, a color, a match, a sunrise!

WOODS AN ART, WINTER

A collection of Poems: Vol XI: A Poetry Classic

Jane Summers

1. Poise, a grace!

My poise,

A grace,

I need seasons!

A grace,

A winter, a huddle,

A cold,

I need to weather!

A winter poise, a warmth, my grace!

A summer poise,

A step, A voice,

A dress, a conversation,

I walk,

For a grace!

An autumn poise,

A task,

My grace, a window ledge, To arrange!

My breeze,

I weather,

An autumn poise, sturdy!

To walk a step for a care,

An autumn poise, a clutch,

My grace!

A spring poise,

I need,

A step light,

A home clean!

An April fresh white blouse, my poise!

My dust mites, moss,

Not any, my blouse!

An April straight, my poise

A poise, true!

A poise seasons, true,

Nature, seasons,

breeze, rain, cold,

Ice, fog, heat,

My poise, seasons!

A poise, seasons true, a grace seasons,

my work only to match a poise!

A flower,

Inside,

An outer petal!

A flower, many, a type,

My inner petals, now,

A celebration,

Awake,

A learning true!

Visible, some,

A sunrise,

Some, a sunset!

Petals, hidden for time, true!

Inner Petals awake, a sunrise, sunset, a difference,

a shape, a learning, a flower many, a type!

3. *Days of bloom, Until!*

A flower, now,

Petals, all, visible,

A bloom,

Until a wither!

Days

I appreciate,

My work,

Fulfilled!

Until a new,

I need to understand,

For a difference!

A new day, a bloom, until a wither, my

learning only for another new!

4. *Petals torn!*

Petals,

A few,

Torn, a breeze, a season!

Nature,

Seasons,

A difference!

A difference

Spring, new, a tear, rain!

Summer, tear, a bee?

Autumn, tear

An autumn dew?

A winter cold, icy, a tear, true!

A tear seasons!

Petals, torn,

A harmony seasons!

A difference,

A demeanor, a person!

A scene, seasons, true

Woods!

Petals torn, seasons breeze or any. A bearing

of a person is dependent upon grace!

5. *Leaves, Spots*

Leaves, spots,

Seasons, a pattern,

A color yellow, spots, a tree!

A pattern,

I need to look at closely!

A fabric, I weave,

A new pattern,

For a difference!

Leaves,

A pattern, seasons,

For a difference!

An autumn, breeze, mist!

For a pattern new!

Winter, a pattern,

Only of a winter pattern, tree and snow!

Ice, a pattern, a difference, a winter, true!

A spring,

A rain,

A pattern, a new leaf!

New, a new bud leaf,

A shape and size, a pattern!

Patterns, new

Seasons,

Any!

Leaves, patterns, several, seasons!

6. *Dance a Season!*

A dance,

A season,

A grace!

Summer,

My dance,

A dance of my flowers,

My leaves,

A summer dance, a baloon!

A summer lilrosea dance!

A dance,

Days,

I need!

Work,

A path,

A difference,

My walk, my dance!

My hands,

My steps,

I need to avoid!

Flares and temper, to replace,

A day of grace,

I need to adorn, every day,

Lest,

My grace lost, true!

A step and hand, a grace, to avoid, a fall, seasons!

7. *Embroidery, a pattern a shade!*

A pattern,

An embroidery,

My garden of roses, daisies,

A difference,

Of a shape,

Shade

And color!

My blouse,

For a difference of

A summer and autumn,

Days of summer,

A summer sunshine,

Yellow and rose!

An autumn deep blue and purple daisies,

An Autumn sun,

An autumn difference!

An embroidery, a difference my dress to

match a summer and an autumn!

8.   *My vase I need to fill!*

A vase empty,

I need to fill!

A pattern,

A flower, a vase,

For a color,

A week, a day,

A season!

A vase,

Empty!

An assortment,

A need, my vase!

A celebration, true,

An assortment!

A fragrance, a need, a season!

A fragrance,

A difference,

A need, a season!

A rose,

My perfume,

For a

harmony!

A lemon,

A thirst to quench,

A summer warm!

A Rosemary,

My kitchen,

A place for friendship!

A lavender,

A balm,

I need for

My aches and pains!

A fragrance,

A difference,

A need

For a health,

And beauty!

9. *A road for a difference!*

A road,

A season,

Strewn of,

Flowers, Leaves,

Any!

Wet, yellow, brown and dry,

A road, days!

A summer road dry,

A fragrance,

My meadows,

Gardenias,

Roses,

Jasmines,

A road, a path clear,

I look at,

A few times, a day

A road

A difference,

For a care,

A fragrance,

My gaze!

A road to look for a difference of an art, and cleanliness, an attitude I wear!

10. *A Flower, afar*

A flower,

Afar,

A summer,

A shape,

A butterfly!

Colors,

Daisies,

Roses,

A pink,

A lavender,

A yellow,

Others!

A butterfly,

Only to seek another,

Of A flower afar, a color

A group,

I belong to!

Mistaken, true?

Only to turn away,

A disappointment!

A need,

To find my own!

A resemblance of a person, my own family.

A need to talk to my own!

11.   *A lamp, a shade!*

A lamp,

A shade,

A night,

A comfort,

A reading, true!

A sleep peaceful

Every!

Lamp,

A purpose, a room,

A difference,

Not any, a room,

A kitchen,

A family room!

A family togetherness,

Only for a harmony,

A conversation,

Only for a family value!

Lamp, a shade, a comfort, a family, a value true!

12.   *A table, a decor*

A table,

A decor,

I need!

An arrangement,

A vase,

A book,

A decor,

An appreciation

Any!

A table,

A corner or any,

I sit,

My work,

My study,

Only for a success!

A table for a need any, I arrange!

13.   A remembrance, I cherish!

A remembrance,

A picture,

Of a person,

A memory,

A lifetime,

My parents!

A gratitude,

A respect,

I pray, every, ever!

A remembrance,

Actions, Sincerity,Trust, a lifetime!

Devotion, a togetherness, every day!

A remembrance,

Stories,

Celebrations,

Birthdays,

Festivals,

A family memory,

A harmony, my mind!

A remembrance, today, afore,

A harmony, seasons,

A lifetime!

A remembrance of parents, teachers, a gratitude,

a respect, I bestow every day, seasons!

14. *Bunches, my torches*

Bunches,

Flowers,

A décor!

A vase, 'O', a crepe myrtle,

A vase my torch, a rose!

A basket, my table,

A basket, my kitchen,

A soup, salad,

My plate, My bowl, my torch!

Bunches, grapes,

A fruit bowl, my vase!

A fruit salad,

An ice cream cup, my torch!

Bunches,

Vegetables, any,

An arrangement, true!

Seasons, any,

A need!

Bunches of torches for an arrangement any!

15. *Leaves, flowers!*

My leaves,

Flowers, every spring,

A flower white, a jasmine,

A flower green, my leaf!

Several,

An arrangement, true!

A day,

Several,

A pattern,

Many,

A branch!

Leaves,

My flowers,

I sew,

A pattern,

An arrangement for!

A new pattern,

A new name, true!

An arrangement for a difference of spring or other seasons!

16. *Pinecone, a rose*

A rose,

Seasons any,

Petals, leaves,

A texture,

Rough,

A pattern!

Jagged, an edge!

A petal,

A shape, rose!

Petals, several,

A rose,

I did not carve!

A rose

I carve,

Of wood,

A difference,

A pinecone rose!

A carve,

A perfection,

Not any a pinecone rose,

Nature,

A carve!

A pattern I did not carve, a carve natural for a difference!

17. *A difference, I am*

Several years,

A home,

I belonged to,

My difference

Now,

Only for a belonging!

A home, my family, now

A joy, ever!

My kitchen,

Only for

A conversation!

A devotion

Of respect,

Sincerity,

Trust

And belonging!

A harmony of

A family togetherness,

Now!

A difference,

Years,

My family,

A need every day!

A difference of before and now, my devotion for sincerity

18. *A bouquet I put together*

Flowers,

An art,

Assembled,

A birthday bouquet!

Flowers, cream,

A sincerity,

My friendship!

My sails of friendship high,

An orchid,

My sails of friendship,

A loyalty, ever!

My marriage poise,

A bouquet!

Yellow and red

My Mums!

White,

My Jasmines!

A color yellow,

Turmeric,

A marriage symbol,

My mangalasutram,

And feet, toe rings!

My bindi, red,

A bride,

On my forehead,

My hair long,

A lifetime, ever!

19.   *A day for others*

A day

Of my visitors,

A day true,

Respect,

A greeting

Of welcome!

A smile

I bestow,

A gesture

For a seat!

A conversation,

Only for smiles,

My visitors!

A beverage,

Food,

I offer!

Only for a liking!

A gift

I bestow,

Only for

A return again!

A visitors, I must treat with respect for a

friendship and a return again!

20. *A leaf that blooms*

A leaf,

A bud

Several days!

Now,

A tiny red,

Not a green,

My wonder!

A yellow,

Another leaf, awake,

My wonder,

A smile,

Not a flower,

A difference

Of a leaf,

Green!

My dress,

A difference

A skirt,

A dress,

A scarf!

A summer dress, light!

An autumn,

A plaid silk,

A petal,

Thickness,

Only for a grace!

A fold,

A fall

More!

A new dress,

Several,

To wear now!

A new name,

A new third-a-season!

Sun-Aut-third!

A difference of a dress, a leaf, a

flower, a skirt and a dress!

21.   *A bud, I drop!*

A bud,

Several days,

I try to unfurl,

Unawake,

Days, night,

Several days a bud!

An illness,

A cure,

A need someone!

I drop, a day

Unknown,

A bud!

A bud dropped,

Several buds,

dropped!

I need a care!

An illness,

For a cure!

Buds,

Now, flowers,

Fragrance, fresh,

A life healthy!

Flowers, fragrance,

A life!

A tree I need to care for, a fragrance, a cure for illness!

22. *A fragrance fresh home, only!*

A fragrance fresh,

My linen!

A house clean, a fragrance!

A fragrance, my dress,

My blues, free!

A fragrance rose faint,

A dress I match,

My spring, summer smiles,

My voice for a

Conversation,

Only for a tone,

Of a cheer,

To match my home!

A fragrance lavender,

A mood,

For my aches and pains,

And a sleep peaceful,

Only for a comfort, true!

A fragrance fresh, my home, a fragrance

fresh every any, for a cheer!

23. *Rolling petals*

Seasons?

An autumn breeze!

Rolling petals,

A fall!

Some a grace,

Some a walk,

A few,

An anger!

A thud, an action!

Not a clap,

Nor A breeze,

Any,

For a Notice,

An appreciation, not any

A caretaker, empty!

Busy,

My days,

My rolling petals, not any I noticed,

Only a stress,

My walk,

My thoughts!

My days of work!

A notice only

Of my work to complete!

An appreciation, true, my work,

A day of my rolling petals, true

My caretaker, true!

Rolling petals, not noticed, until a work fulfilled!

24. *A farm, A need!*

A farm,

Not any,

My pots,

I grow,

Tomatoes,

Carrots,

Radish!

A need, I need to,

A farm,

My plants,

I tend to,

Water, soil, every!

A few, I survive,

A color, true,

My carrots, radishes,

I learnt,

My tomatoes, bean stalks,

A learning

I need,

Every, a farm!

Learnt, a season,

A farm,

To learn, all,

A need, true!

25. *Leaves, a spill*

Leaves,

A few, a spill,

Mangoes,

A bunch a spill, rain, true!

Lotus,

Leaves,

A few, a spill,

A lake,

A step, not now!

Banana leaves,

A spill,

A mid-summer

Drops,

I count!

A drop,

A few,

Several

New words,

Names,

I relate to others,

A learning true,

My drops!

Leaves a spill a season, a need, for

a difference of a new word.

26. *A cluster of flowers*

A cluster of flowers,

A beauty,

A difference, days!

A flower,

A fold,

A size,

A shape,

A color,

Sunrise, sunset!

Only for an appreciation!

27. *A gathering, a need!*

A gathering,

A crowd, a festival, a year,

Mourning, a sadness, a few!

A gathering, every day,

Only a disturbance!

A task,

Every, a season,

A person, I am

Responsible, my actions,

My work,

My devotion,

A sincerity true!

A gathering only

For a recognition!

A celebration,

A meeting, true!

A gathering is not a need always, a few a joy!

WOODS AN ART, SPRING

A Collection of Poems: Vol

XII – A Poetry Classic

Jane Summers

1. *Lines, a pattern!*

A bud,

Inverted,

Faint lines,

Petals,

A lavender skirt,

A pattern!

A circle,

Ellipses,

And Splashes,

A pattern, a vase!

An inverted flower a pattern of a skirt with faint line, a bluebell!

2. *A Zigzag, a pattern!*

A Zigzag

A pattern,

A leaf stitch!

Several, a leaf,

A season!

Spring,

Summer,

A zigzag leaf, true!

Autumn,

Zig zag stitches, worn!

A Winter,

Not any,

Bare, a vase !

A zigzag pattern,

A leaf, any,

For time!

Until,

A new!

A zigzag,

A new leaf,

A perennial, true!

A zigzag pattern, a stitch, a zigzag, visible,

A summer, worn, a winter!

3. *A Dot, a Pattern*

A dot a pattern

Several now,

A leaf!

A pattern, true,

Rain, mist

A dot, true?

Not any for time now?

Several dots, a leaf,

A color, two, now!

Until rain!

Not any,

A pattern now!

A dot, several dots, rain,

A match, a dot, a leaf!

Dots, a pattern of leaves, trees!

A pattern, a season all?

Dots, a pattern several leaves, an autumn or a late summer!

4. *Shapes, A Pattern*

A round,

A shape, a moon!

A pattern, a moon, an inner!

Yellow, irises!

A pattern,

Round,

Apples, peaches,

Fruits, many!

For time,

Until, a season new,

A new pattern, true!

New, a full moon,

119

A pattern new!

A star,

A pattern,

Until time,

A match, true!!

A moon a pattern a match fruits, a color, shape. A star a pattern, a match, a full moon, a time!

5. Star, A Pattern

Stars,

A pattern, a night, true!

Clouds, seasons,

a pattern, true!

A triangle,

Several, a star, a pattern!

A rangoli,

My star pattern!

A decoration, a star,

A Christmas tree!

Stars, a pattern several a night!

6.   *A line, a middle!*

A leaf,

A line,

A middle,

A pattern, true!

A middle,

A center, a half-pattern, true!

A leaf, a side, a pattern, true!

A leaf new, a pattern,

Until, a new pattern,

A new leaf, true!

A leaf, lines several, a pattern true! A mid-point, a leaf, a new pattern true!

7. Lines, parallel!

Lines, parallel,

Several, a leaf!

A mid-point, a half!

A line,

A match,

A side, a leaf, true!

Lines, faint, a leaf,

Distinct, a pattern, rain,

Ice, Snow,

Not any!

Another,

Only for a season, new!

Lines parallel, a leaf, a pattern, true!

8. *Lines, a Step!*

Lines,

A step,

An edge, a border,

A leaf!

A step new,

Not A difference, any!

Similar, a shape, seasons!

A difference,

I subtract,

Up or down!

A pattern,

A step,

A temple pattern,

A temple border, a pattern,

My saree,

A temple pattern, my saree

I wear!

A pattern, an arc, a leaf, a temple pattern, An edge, a leaf!

9. *Stone, a Pattern!*

Stones, Many,

A Pattern!

A stone,

A pattern,

Jagged!

A smooth, several lines, a pattern!

A pattern, A shape,

A home, any!

Marbles, a pattern,

A decor,

any!

Stones, a rough edge, a pattern,

A gravel, a path!

A stone,

A use,

Any, a season!

Not a difference,

For Time!

Stones, a pattern many, a stone a purpose, a use!

10. Colors, A Pattern

A stone, any,

Color, a pattern!

A pattern,

Light,

A pattern of spots,

A pattern, dark,

A difference of,

A new color,

A new Shape,

A new pattern!

A new color pattern,

A new name, true!

Colors of shapes, a color, a spot, a new pattern,

11.   *A pattern, an idol!*

A pattern,

An idol,

A temple!

Several shapes, an art, true!

An idol,

A round,

An angle, a hollow!

Lines, a pattern

For a standing or

A sitting posture!

A stone, an idol several patterns. A pattern, a shape a God Idol

12. *Carrots, a shape*

Carrots,

long, a, stalk,

A head, a head

A pattern!

Colors, many a carrot,

A color

A difference, a pattern!

An orange, a pink,

Any, a pattern!

A carrot,

A size,

A color,

Patterns, many!

Carrots, many a shape, a color, a type, a head!

13. *My braid Pattern*

A flower arrangement, atop, my head!

A shape, a pattern,

Similar a carrot!

Color, a difference, a braid!

Flowers white, atop head

A white, green and orange,

My braid!

A carrot braid, true!

A braid several patterns a weave, an art true!

14.   *A bow, several patterns!*

A bow,

A pattern many?

A silk!

A shape, many

A size,

A silk bow!

A green,

A color for time,

Now, a yellow,

A dry grass,

A brown,

Not for, A wither!

A carrot green bow,

A pattern,

A decor,

My table,

An arrangement, many,

A pattern!

Carrot heads several patterns, a color, a bow, a size!

15. *Parsley, a pattern*

Parsley,

Leaves, green,

A pattern!

A leaf complete, a pattern new!

A decor in my kitchen pot,

My window ledge,

A kitchen pattern!

Herbs,

A fragrance,

My kitchen,

Seasons!

A pattern,

A difference,

An autumn!

A plaid,

My kitchen pot,

A match,

My plant, pattern!

Parsley, a herb, a pattern, a head, a stalk, A fragrance, a kitchen!

16. *A pattern, palms*

Palms, a pattern,

A wide, a leaf,

Edges, a pattern!

Several a shape, a palm leaf,

A pattern!

Leaves, a pattern,

An art, many!

Palms,

A pattern for a use,

A plate!

An arrangement

In a vase,

A pattern!

Several halves,

A palm leaf

A pattern, true!

Palms, a pattern a half, a full, asize, a color for a use!

17. *A rock, a pattern*

A rock,

A pattern, an ocean,

Lines parallel, a wave, a rock,

A morning sunrise,

A rock, a lingam!

A sunset rock,

sunset lines,

A pattern!

A color,

A size,

A home!

A difference, sunrise, sunset!

A rock, a pattern in an ocean, A difference

of a sunrise and sunset!

18.   *A pattern, my hand!*

A pattern,

Several, my palm,

A difference,

A palm!

Patterns, lines

A path, a difference of time,

For a path!

Patterns, a difference,

For a path, similar!

A pattern, several, a palm,

An arch,

A bridge, a cross-cross,

An intersection, a pattern!

Lines, zigzag,

Similar, Rocks,

A pattern!

A pattern, a palm several, a cross-cross, a line,

a zig zag and others, a use to make any!

19.   *A pattern, a maple leaf*

A pattern,

Three a lobe, a leaf petal,

An arc,

Not similar!

A petal leaf,

A color deep

Lines, similar,

A line, a shape,

A difference!

A maple leaf petal,

Another?

A harmony, true!

A maple syrup,

Cookie,

A pattern,

A match, a maple leaf!

My maple cookie

Patterns,

Several,

A match,

A difference,

A new maple leaf,

An autumn!

A pattern, a leaf, a three lobe, a symbol,

to make a napkin, and others.

20. *Honeysuckle, a pattern*

A pattern, my flowers,

Honeysuckle,

An ellipse, a petal pattern!

A star,

A hollow,

A triangle,

Sizes, many,

A pattern, true!

Several ellipses,

A size,

A pattern, true!

Flowers, honeysuckle,

A sunrise pattern,

A difference,

A sunset, pattern!

Honeysuckle, leaves, several a pattern, A use to make a craft!

21. A fallen petal!

22.   *A garland, a pattern!*

A garland,

A pattern, I sew,

A color, a plaid,

A pattern!

A color yellow,

Mums and roses,

A pattern!

A braid

3 a line

Until 2 and

One,

A new pattern!

Leaves, A color many,

a new pattern,

Leaf-A-Summer Pattern!

Garlands, several a pattern an occasion!

23. An arrangement flowers, a pattern

Several flowers,

An arrangement, a line,

A line, Jasmine's, a four, a stitch,

A line, a kanakambaram,

A 5 a stitch, until 20, a line!

A round, Roses, Atop,

A stitch,

For a bun!

A pattern,

A basket weave,

A flower handle, atop,

To hold!

Flowers a pattern for an arrangement, a sew!

24. *A basket, a pattern*

Baskets,

Several a pattern,

A pattern, a

A jute!

A weave horizontal,

A pattern,

A basket,

A weave, a vertical,

A basket a laundry basket, an art true!

A yarn, a pattern,

Several

Shapes, sizes

A new fabric

A weave!

A pattern, a yarn type, a jute, a wood, cloth

and others for a difference!

25. *A pattern, a song*

Songs,

Notes, a pattern, many!

A note higher,

A pattern,

A note lower,

A new!

A note,

A serene,

A pattern calm,

Higher, lower, serene!

A tone,

A pattern!

A pattern,

Songs,

notes

Many,

Seasons,

A difference,

A note

I choose!

Songs, notes a pattern, a difference of seasons, I choose!

26. *A pattern, a look!*

Patterns, many, a hair style,

A hair down

A pattern!

Buns many,

A formal pattern!

A hair, a criss-cross,

A pattern!

A hair,

To the side,

A pattern!

Hair bunched on top,

A pattern!

A patternlet art, any, true!

A hairstyle, many a pattern true, an artlet!

27. *A distortion, a pattern!*

A name

Unknown,

A distortion!

A disarray,

A shirt,

Loose, several sizes, a disarray!

A patternlet art, distorted!

A disheveled arrangement,

A pant!

Hair?

An unkempt clothing, any

All, a distortion!

A pattern, a disarray,

For a use?

Oh yes!

A scarecrow celebration,

An autumn!

A pumpkin festival, true!

A disarray for a use, a celebration, true!

WOODS AN ART, SUMMER

A Collection of Poems: Vol XIII: A Poetry Classic

Jane Summers

1. *Points to Synonyms met!*

Points to synonyms met,

Activity points, a measure!

Features, similar,

A synonym, a point!

To combine

Similarities,

Using

Lines, similar,

A point value!

A

Synonym study,

A similarity new,

a difference, approach!

A new definition,

A new learning,

A new synonym, true!

An empirical map of a synonym,

A parallelism, true!

Points to synonym, to determine more

synonyms from a difference of any!

2. *Combinacrique, a Methodology!*

A critique,

To combine,

Present, past, a new abstraction,

An abstraction,

To a value, combined,

A new critique!

A methodology, to combine,

for a translation,

Time Trend,

An angle, true!

An angle,

A relationship,

To combine,

Or create,

A method,

A comparison, true,

A Critique,

I write!

A critique I combine for a value, an angle a

difference of an old, for a new value!

3. *A Curvy ivy, An abstraction*

A Curvy, ivy, many, a season,

A map, a theory,

A theory of ivy curves,

Not similar, any a curve!

A point, a fact, a translation,

Several ivy theories, facts, examples!

Reasons, a proof, true!

A Rule methodology met!

A curvy parallelism,

A map several, similar

A result,

A method,

Single,

A map!

A curvy ivy theory, a map of several ivy curves for a theory!

4. *Disquisition!*

An abstraction,

For A disquisition!

A study of a subject,

A comprehensive

Note, my disquisition!

Creativity, A support,

To translate,

My paragraph,

An Overview for a disquisition!

A disquisition, a difference,

of my essay,

Notes,

A collection,

A new disquisition, true!

An abstract disquisition, true!

A disquisition, a note or an overview, a

collection for a new abstraction!

5. *A wave abstraction*

An abstraction

For a wave of definitions,

Several,

I compare.

For a definition, true!

A wave, a relation of time,

New waves, a new definition,

An extension, existing,

A time to relate!

Several new waves,

A new abstract, true, a wave!

A wave of terms for usage, is a time factor

to derive new, and existing!

6. *Requirements Subtraction theory*

An abstraction

Of a requirement,

A statement,

An action,

Only for a value!

A requirement subtraction,

A requirement difference,

A difference,

Only for time!

A requirement subtraction,

For an improvement,

An urgency,

A value of time!

A requirement subtraction theory, a value, time!

A requirement subtraction, a difference for time!

7. *Practices Maximization abstract theory*

An abstraction,

Practices,

Any,

A use,

A purpose,

I maximize,

A standardization for use,

I choose!

A return,

A use,

Only for a maximization, true!

Practices in any area for implementation

to return a maximized value.

8.   *Constraint fulfillment abstract theory*

An abstract,

A constraint,

A goal,

A rule to fulfill,

A constraint,

I accommodate!

A tax,

A constraint,

For a home,

I own,

A payment,

I fulfill!

A save,

Met,

A tax fulfillment met!

A constraint, any,

Only to meet, a need, true!!

Constraint fulfillment only for a need!

9. Constraint limitation theory

A constraint,

I minimize,

For a

Goal to fulfill!

A constraint,

I am aware,

A limitation,

I cannot

Go beyond,

A constraint,

I met,

As part of my rule,

A use, a purpose!

A goal met!

A constraint to minimize for an optimal value, true!

10. *In-Decisiveness translate Value theory*

An abstraction,

An Indecision,

A set of statements,

Rules,

I need to translate, quickly,

A decision for a value,

A translation value for,

A Maximization!

An indecision,

A wastage,

A process,

I translate to,

Rules for Value and Wastage

A fulfillment for!

A decision value, true!

An indecisiveness I translate to a value for

a decision of value through rules.

11.   *Pick continuity theory*

A continuity theory,

I pick,

A rule wasted,

For a new!

A return true,

A util,

A value, true

My pick!

A continuity theory,

Not any a waste,

A process,

A use,

A purpose,

For a continue,

Until, true!

A continuity theory I pick, a value to continue

until a purpose, wasted is true!

12. *Commit-to-deliver-Core Theory*

A commit to deliver,

For a core result,

An action,

To meet, a commit,

A goal,

Several

Statements,

I fulfill!

A competency,

An action,

To match,

A skill met,

To delivery,

A fulfillment true!

A commit-to-deliver,

Core theory, true!

A commitment to delivery must match a

commitment for a delivery fulfilled.

13. *Values-util-deficient theory*

Values,

For a purpose,

Not any

For an under utlilization,

A value,

For a

Purpose, a return

Tangible, intangible,

A cost,

A factor of Utils derived,

An Optimization,

Utils, true,

Marginal, a util,

Not any,

Deficient,

A value!

Under-utilized!

A util value

Not met!

A utilization value to be met for a value and utils

derived per util cost value translated.

WOODS, AN ART, WINTER

A Collection of Poems: Vol IIX: A poetry Classic

Jane Summers

1. *Pensacious Woods!*

My woods,

A few days, a season,

A solitude,

Pensacious!

An autumn,

My woods,

My days of work,

A learilligent, true!

Art,

Celebrations,

An appreciation for!

memories,

To cherish,

A lifetime!

True,

A pensiciousness,

Sacred!

Woods, a solitude, a few days, a season, Pensacious true!

2. Woods, an Auteaceset, true!

Autumn woods,

An autumn peaceful, a sunset!

My autumn woods,

Auteaceset, true!

Only beautiful,

More, an autumn,

Every day!

An auteaceset beautiful an autumn, orange and white a sky!

3. *Autreezerise Woods!*

An autreezrise,

A day of,

Woods,

A décor!

Only to Autrrange,

An arrangement sacred!

An arrangement,

Of a breeze,

A difference, a decor, days of autumn,

An autivy weave, one, true!

An autreezrise,

Beautiful, an autumn

Only, gracious!

An autreezrise, days of autumn, a difference, a décor!

4. *Autriseprayers*

My Autriseprayers,

An autumn, a sunrise,every,

Peacilent!

My autriseprayers,

Only for

An autumn day!

Not a breeze,

Any for an illness!

A warmth,

Only

My family,

A comfort,

My home!

My autriseprayers, an autumn a comfort my family!

5. *Autumn Autorlon!*

Woods,

This Autumn,

Autorlon,

Not any,

A visitor!

Tis autumn,

Only an

Auteezrise,

My visitor!

Autorlon,

Days of autumn,

Flowers,

A dance

Of a forlorn day,

A difference,

An Autorlon dance,

Precious,

An autumn!

My days of autumn, a few, autorlon, only

for a breeze, sunrise, my visitors!

6. *Autfestlessings*

An autumn

Festival,

Every autumn,

Holy,

Sacred,

An autumn!

My autfestlessings,

True!

A celebration,

My autrise,

Mu autumn pumpkins, only true!

7. *Autacred!*

An autumn,

A day of a month,

Sacred to

Perform,

A pooja, my, tree!

My autumn day,

Autacred!

Sacred,

My words

Of pooja,

A fast, not to eat!

To arrange,

My God, sacred!

A respect,

My customs!

autacred,

A day, true!

Autacred, my days of pooja, an autumn day!

8. *Beaulligent!*

Holy,

Sacred,

Only Beaulligent,

Studies, work,

A poise!

My work,

A walk of life!

A name

I call thee,

A gracelligent!

Intelligent,

And graceful,

A use,

A purpose,

Worthy!

9. *An Autumn floweracious!*

My autumn roses, flowers,

Floweracious!

Autumn,

My days,

Only more graceful,

My autumn trees,

My autumn woods!

10. *Autuarm!*

Autarm,

My autumn home!

Autumn

Pumpkin-cinnamon buns,

Autumn tea, rich!

An autumn warmth,

My autumn,

Velvet blanket,

A comfort,

A corner!

Autarm,

My autumn days,

Not Autorlon!

11. *Autew*

My autew,

A day of

White mist,

Several visitors,

Passed by!

Afar!

A soft breeze,

A whisper,

A walk of several,

A grace,

A March

Of a breeze,

A grey!

A hand,

Only

A need,

A mist, to clear,

My eyes, wet

A search for a path,

Ahead, an autumn,

A day,

Of an

Autew, true!

PRAYERS OF GRATITUDE

Prayers of gratitude,

A sunrise morning!

Every day,

For a day of work, I do,

Gratitude, my day, fulfilled!

A gratitude,

My health,

A blessing, true!

A day of prayers,

Sunrise, sunset,

A gratitude,

To my,

Parents, teachers,

My path, a road one, harmony!

Memories of advice,

I cherish,

For a use, a purpose, every day!

A blessing, my life!

A gratitude,

My life,

My food,

shelter,

Any,

A gratitude,

I bestow, ever!

Prayers of gratitude, for any and every, I fulfill!

Word	Meaning and Sentence
Pensacious	Pensive and gracious: *My autumn pumpkins are pensive and gracious an autumn early sunrise!*
Autew	Autew: Autumn Dew *My autew mist, a cloak, an autew flower!*
Autrise	Autumn Sunrise *An autrise, for blessings of God, an autumn prayer, an autrise, true!*
Auteaceset	Autumn Peaceful Sunset *An Auteaceset, peaceful and solemn, a few days!*
Autfestlessings	Autumn festival blessings *My Autfestlessings, a day of Dasara, a holy day, one a year, a celebration!*
Autacred	Autumn sacred *An autumn sacred, every, an autumn festival!*
Beaulligent	Beauty and Intelligence *She is very beaulligent!*
Autracious	Autumn Gracious *An autracious, My birch tree, every autumn!*
Dilligelligence	Diligence and Intelligence *She is very dilligelligence in her work*
Autreezrise	Autreezrise *An autumn breeze sunrise, I look at, every day, a difference of an ordinary!*

PART 2 – VOCAL SONGS

Summer Sunrise

Summer Sun,

Sunrise Every summer!

Summer Sun,

Sunset, Every Evening!

Seasons, Summers Seasons,

Summer Seasons,

Summer Seasons

Paragraph1:

Leaves and flowers,

A dance of sunrise, true!

Buds and Dew,

A dance of sunset, true!

Seasons, Summers Seasons,

Summer Seasons,

Summer Seasons

Paragraph 2:

Clouds and Mist,

A day of autumn, True!

Sun and Moon,

A dance of sunshine, true!

Seasons, Summers Seasons,

Summer Seasons,

Summer Seasons

Repeat:

Summer Sun,

Sunrise Every summer!

Summer Sun,

Sunset, Every Evening!

Seasons, Summers Seasons,

Summer Seasons,

S-u-m-m-er S-e-a-s-o-n-s!

NEW LANGUAGE - DURVUE

Alphabets				
English	**Durvue**	**Pronunciation**	**English**	**Durvue**
A	Aue	Aau	And	Anuve
B	Bue	Bau	Is	Sovue
C	Cue	Cau	Are	Arvue
D	Due	Dau	For	Fovue
E	Eue	Eau	Forgone	Forvue

F	Fue	Fau	Go	Govue
H	Hue	Hau	Myself	Mesovue
I	Iue	Iau	Beautiful	Beouvue
J	Jue	Jau	Sincere	Sieovue
K	Kue	Kau	Sacred	Sacovue
L	Lue	Lau	Trust	Trusovue
M	Mue	Mau	Forever	Foveoue
N	Nue	Nau	because	bevovue
O	Oue	Oau	Autumn	Aumovue
P	Pue	Pau	Summer	Sumovue
Q	Que	Qau	Spring	Sprovue
R	Rue	Rau	Winter	Winvoue
S	Sue	Sau	Day	Daovuen
T	Tue	Tau	Of	Ovue
U	Uue	Uau	Not	Novue
V	Vue	Vau	Any	Anovue
W	Wue	Wau	Only	Onovue
X	Xue	Xau	To	Tovue
Y	Yue	Yau	Time	Tiouve
Z	Zue	Zau	Miss	Misouve
			My	Mivue
			Carve	Cavoue
			An	Aoue
			Art	Arovue

Anue Aumovue Forvue (An Autumn Foregone)

My days of autumn,

Mivue Daovuen Ovue Aumovue,

Not any,

Novue Anovue,

A Time,

Aue Tiouve,

To miss

Tovue Misouve,

An art,

Auve Arovue,

Lest,

Lesovue

A day forgone!

Aue Daovuen Forvue

Printed in the United States
by Baker & Taylor Publisher Services